This book belongs to

. . . .

for Marie and Jess

P.M.

for my sister Louise

S.B.

Text copyright © Paula Metcalf 2014

Illustrations copyright © Suzanne Barton 2014

The rights of Paula Metcalf to be identified as the Author and Suzanne Barton to be identified
as the Illustrator of this Work have been asserted by them in accordance with the
Copyright, Designs and Patent Act, 1988 (United Kingdom).

This edition published in 2016

First published in hardback in Great Britain in 2014 by words & pictures
Part of The of Quarto Group
The Old Brewery, 6 Blundell Street, London N7 9BH

British Library Cataloguing in Publication Data available on request

ISBN: 978-1-91027-716-4

1 3 5 7 9 8 6 4 2

Printed in China

A Guide to Sisters

to

Sisters

Paula Metcalf

Illustrations by Suzanne Barton

words & pictures

Contents

Introduction

If you're thinking about getting a sister or
you want to understand one you already have,
this guide is for you.

1. Starting off

Sisters come in two sizes:

big and little.

Most of the time, you get a
new sister from hospital.
They are warm and squishy,
like a freshly-baked loaf of bread . . .
but you do NOT put butter on them.

Also, they're a lot noisier.

"Waaahh!"

Sometimes, they do Buy One Get One Free.

"WAAAAAHHH!"

"aah!"

Little sisters are very busy.
They cry, eat, sleep, produce
dirty nappies and cry some more.
But, to make it all worthwhile,
they give sweet baby kisses!

And then their teethies
come along. Teeny,
adorable . . .
. . . *sharp* teethies.

"OUCH!"

2. On the Move

One of the many joys awaiting big sisters is when little sist
learn to walk, and can go every-single-place with them.

"Weeeeeeeee!"

(Lots of places have handy 'holders
to store little sisters while big sister
get on with their important busines

3. Cuteness

There is nothing as irresistible as a little sister! They are so cute that they have to get picked up, kissed and whirled around many times each day.

Luckily, big sisters don't have to go through all that.

4. A Gift

Mummies say, "a sister is the greatest gift a person can receive." (When they say this, they mean she's a gift for *you* . . . NOT that you should give her away at the next birthday party you go to!)

5. Fun and Games

Little sisters are happiest when they're pressing buttons.
Their favourite button is the one that switches the TV
on and off,

       on and off,

              on and off and

                     on and off.

"STOP THAT!"

Sometimes, big sisters wish that little sisters had an on and off button, too.

6. Tickling

This cut-out-and-keep handy reminder shows
the main ticklish spots of the little sister.

Little sisters can be wiggly so, for best results,
secure them to the floor like so:

fig: 3

7. Style

Some have it ...   ... some don't.

Big sisters have to wait until their 7th birthday before they're allowed to wear high heels.

Little sisters have to wait until their big sister's 7th birthday before *they're* allowed to wear heels.

8. Clothes

If little sisters dress themselves, it's best
to check them before they leave
the house.

"Your shoes are on the wrong feet!"

"No, they're not! These are MY feet!"

"What are you wearing under your coat?"

9. Make-up

Big sisters are allowed to wear a bit of lip gloss and nail polish. Little sisters are not.

But who needs make-up . . .

. . . when there are markers?

10. Sharing

Little sisters are really good at sharing.

They share your sweets, your toys, your clothes . . .

Big sisters are really good at sharing, too.

"One for you, two for me . . ."

11. Making stuff

Anything a little sister can do, a big sister can do better.

Big sisters can make a princess' bed out of two
cereal boxes, four toilet roll tubes and an old towel.

Little sisters can make a princess' toilet out of the broken yogurt pot that wasn't needed for the princess' bed.

Little sisters can also make two cereal boxes, four toilet roll tubes and an old towel out of a princess' bed.

12. Tidying Up

Keeping things neat can be fun. Big sisters! Try this simple game. Time your little sister to see how long it takes her to pick up all clothing, games, books and toys from your bedroom floor and put them where they belong.

Watch how happy she is each week as she tries
to be faster than she was the week before!

13. Bedtime

When night comes, it's time to put aside all the fighting of the day and be kind to each other.

What a great feeling! Drifting off to sleep knowing
that the person who knows you better than anyone
else is so near.

Your friend, your midnight buddy, the greatest gift
you can ever receive . . .

your sister!

P.S. Little sisters can sometimes get scared in the middle of the night. So can big sisters.